A WORKING FAMILY'S GUIDE TO TRUTH IN AN AGE OF UNBELIEVABLE LIES, CONS, AND DISINFORMATION

by

George Lucaci

DORRANCE
PUBLISHING CO
EST. 1920
PITTSBURGH, PENNSYLVANIA 15238

Dorrance Publishing Co
585 Alpha Drive
Pittsburgh, PA 15238
Visit our website at *www.dorrancebookstore.com*

ISBN: 978-1-6491-3169-0
eISBN: 978-1-6491-3674-9

CONTENTS

Chapter 1

INTRODUCTION

"Leadership consists of nothing but taking responsibility for everything that goes wrong and giving your subordinates credit for everything that goes well."

– Dwight D. Eisenhower

Every few years, when I visit my childhood neighborhood on the west side of Cleveland, I am reminded of the October evening touch football games. We played by houses built so close to each other that we couldn't distinguish whose black-and-white T.V. was blaring. This was decades before email, cell phones, or voice mail. These games always extended into the darkness. When the streetlights came on, our mothers called us in for bedtime, each voice distinct. It was a time when civil rights and voting rights were being debated, the sexual revolution was yet to be, and a war hero named Ike led us into global leadership. Americans were proud of their leaders. Now, the leaders of that same party desperately need to find redemption, so their obituaries won't shame their grandchildren. They need to find their souls.

Below the surface of this Norman Rockwell imagery was the ugly remnants of Jim Crow laws manifested by thoroughly segregated neighborhoods and schools. African American economic and social disenfranchisement was still in full force, and many of the new immigrants, like my parents, were from Eastern Europe. The 1965 March from Selma to Montgomery was yet to happen, and we were still catching up with the Russians in the race to the Moon. Nevertheless, we called ourselves a democracy, we were proud, and we believed in a better future.

It was also a time when a postal worker and hairdresser could put three children through college without a lifetime of debt—a time when the college dream was real, not the undoing of a whole generation of Americans. *Saturday Night Live*'s 37-year-old Colin Jost in a March 16, 2020, article in *The New Yorker* stated, "My grandfather worked four jobs. He was a fireman, a handyman, a substitute teacher, and a house painter. With those jobs, he was able to put four children through college."

The unsustainable burden that college debt is playing in contemporary American life is one of the many reasons millennials have lost their patience with a Washington corrupted by too many baby boomers who have unwittingly sold their souls and ignored the morality taught by their parents. They put their hope in an extreme narcissist, who continues to hammer and bruise our democratic institutions with impunity. The honest, hardworking family is being conned by an amoral man with a sense of reality so distorted that they will not endure another four years and survive.

Who is the working family? It's the 23-year-old mother from East Los Angeles playing with her nine-month-old son in the morning before going to work at the local AutoZone. It's National Park Service workers, the emergency staff at so many hospitals throughout this country, the border patrol agents waking before dawn, the young black couple living in Chicago's west side working two jobs each, the jazz drummer from Manhattan's East Village, and the couple with three children struggling to pay rent on their row house in East Baltimore. It's the maintenance men cleaning up the shopping centers in North Palm Beach, Florida; Paramus, New Jersey; El Paso, Texas; or Columbus, Ohio. It's the debt-burdened college dropout, working two shifts on weekends at the Pit-N-Patio pizza parlor in Rhode Island. It's also the restaurant workers, grocery store employees, cashiers, nurses, truck drivers, and all those who make up the front line of defense against the COVID-19 virus. Finally, it's every underpaid teacher working past the last bell, using his or her personal time to tutor those students falling behind, and now scrambling around the clock to adjust the curriculum to remote teaching.

Many years ago, my wife and children began our yearly Easter trek to St. Bartholomew's Cathedral in New York. Their weekly bulletin inspired me with two simple paragraphs titled "What We're For," "an open-minded and passionate commitment to truth," and "What We're Against." This second paragraph rang true for me because it aptly described our current leadership in Washington, D.C.: "Claiming to have all the answers…Bigotry for any reason. Indifference to injustice and suffering. Certitude in the face of ambiguity, and superficial answers to hard questions." So simple, yet sadly so descriptive of our present-day leadership.

Both working-class and middle-class citizens should be angry because they are being deceived by a White House demagogue and an enabling Senate majority leader. Both operate on a platform of discrimination, bigotry, and cultural divide. They are very near completing the balkanization of America. The punchline is that increasing inequality elected Donald Trump, but in their desperation, they let the wolf in the hen house. (See the T.E.D. talk called "Beware, fellow plutocrats, the pitchforks are coming," by Nick Hanauer, August 2014.)

In essence, the working man and woman took the bait. They are now falling even further into economic oblivion. It is time they understand why they were conned and to know how much further they can fall. They need to start asking more questions instead of blindly following a man who they believe represents their frustration and anger. Finally, they need to demand that the American enterprise system serves them and that it should be a force for the betterment of their lives.

RealClear Opinion Research in a recent poll showed 84 percent of Americans believe "the country is run by an alliance of politicians and elites for their own gain." This transcends all generations. In fact, "government ethics and corruption" was listed as number one of the 25 topics in the survey, which included healthcare and crime.

This is not an economic or statistical treatise on inequality or the ever-increasing income gap between the top 1 percent and everybody else. It is a simple guide or roadmap for the vast majority of Americans who need to regain their honor as productive individuals and who have been alienated by globalization, automation, and the outsourcing of American jobs.

Ray Dalio, the founder of Bridgewater, the largest hedge fund in the world, illustrates the plight and evolution of the working family in America: "The wealth of the top one-tenth of 1% of the population is about equal to that of the bottom 90% of the population, which is the same sort of wealth gap that existed during the 1935-40 period." Ray Dalio illustrates this from the NBER Working Paper Series by Emmanuel Saez and Gabriel Zucman, October 2014.

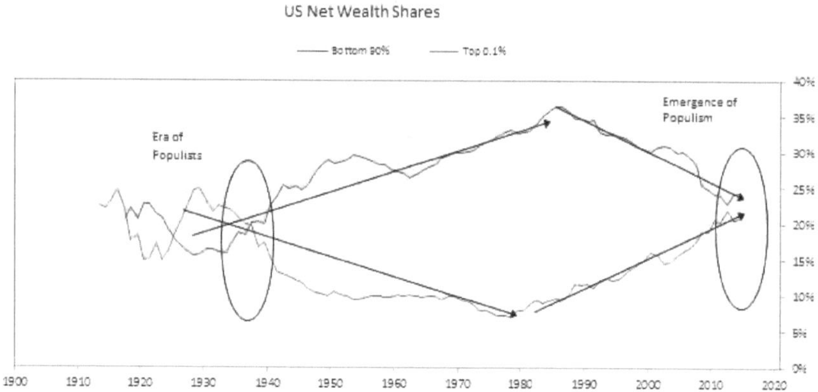

It should also be noted that those states where automotive assembly plants were closed for at least five years had a significantly higher rate of deaths from opioid overdoses than those states where auto assembly plants remained open. (JAMA Intern Med., published online December 30, 2019). There is also a crisis in our country with what some would call "deaths of despair," that is, suicide levels that surpass all our fellow Western democracies and are more akin to Russia and the former Soviet Union.

Despite the administration touting job creation and a strong economy, the average American's life expectancy is dropping, we continue to lose manufacturing jobs, and farm bankruptcies were up 20 percent in 2019. Our country is now in a pandemic-created depression, and opioid addiction and suicide among the working poor and middle class will only accelerate. The rural-urban divide will become America's open sore.

This short guide is for Americans who want to be part of a rapidly changing technologically driven economy. It is for the young who have fallen behind the expectation of doing better than their parents. It is for the older generation who no longer has the skills to be part of an economy that has little similarity to what existed just 20 years ago. But it is especially so for those who have too often voted against their economic interests.

This is about the inextricable link between democracy, capitalism, and economic fairness, and how all three can co-exist for the betterment of the working family. Finally, it is meant to be a short guide for the majority of Americans who have become lost politically, economically, and socially by what used to be the party of Lincoln.

LIES! HOAX!
WITCH HUNT!
DOESN'T THAT HURT YOUR BACKBONE?
MY WHAT?
WASSERMAN © 11.19
DIST. BY TRIBUNE CONTENT AGENCY
www.bostonglobe.com/wasserman

Chapter 2
THE GREAT AMERICAN MAGIC ACT

"The forest was shrinking, but the trees kept voting for the ax. For the ax was clever and convinced the trees that because his handle was wood, he was one of them."

– West Asian Fable

The famous French author Baudelaire wrote, "The devil's cleverest wile is to make men believe that he does not exist." The greatest trick Donald Trump ever pulled was convincing the working families of America that he could improve their lot in life. Sadly, and just as illusionary, the greatest trick the Democrats ever pulled was convincing their core constituency that Trump couldn't win.

Both of these charades were played out in a chaotic circus tent known as our democratic process with the mainstream media as our feckless master of ceremonies. Never was there any real analysis of the need to reshape our economic models. Through a bit of black magic, Trump managed to stay in the center ring as the freak show star. His well-intentioned loyalists, wanting better lives, are still suffering even more than before his election. The tents have been folded for nearly four years. Yet, according to the latest census data, half of Americans can still be considered poor or low income, and homeownership itself has become a luxury. Young adults today are less likely to own a home than their parents, as too many are saddled with crippling student debt, and African American homeownership has fallen to its lowest level in 60 years.

Today, one in five adults is unable to pay the current month's bills, and the pandemic will double that most recent statistic. Unexpected home repair bills or a sick child with an emergency room medical expense would be catastrophic without health insurance when almost 9 percent of Americans went without health insurance in 2019. Now, with millions out of work because of the pandemic, that percentage will soar. Yet a tiny percentage of Americans have accumulated enormous wealth while one in three households are classified as "financially fragile," which means they would struggle to come up with $500 for an unexpected expense. That expense will most likely be medical.

Regretfully, neither party had a real plan for the working family. But it was President Trump who created and nourished the narrative of fear and hate with incredible and constant lies. He instinctively exploited the white man's fear of independent and liberated women, as well as growing religious and racial minorities. This fear, along with the spread of disinformation and the licensing of extreme bigotry, gave legitimacy and power to the most extreme, hate-filled, and paranoid elements of society.

The working family will not be ready to reestablish a new American dream unless they also lead the fight against racism, political corruption, mass incarceration, an unjust healthcare system, and a tax system that continues to increase income inequality. Our poorest states, like Alabama, Mississippi, West Virginia, Louisiana, and New Mexico, still have strong net approvals for our current president despite statistics that show that there has been no improvement in their healthcare or income.

When the middle- and working-class votes against their interests, it has a broader social, economic, and even cultural impact. We are now seeing the social dislocations and unrest from these self-inflicted wounds evidenced by a study conducted by the Harvard School of Medicine and Cambridge Health Alliance that says 45,000 people die each year due to lack of health insurance. The link between lackluster wage growth and the ravages of the opium epidemic and suicides has been well established by numerous studies. (Opioid Crisis: No Easy Fix to Its Social and Economic Determinants, Am J Public Health. 2018 February;108(2):182-186)

When your representative tells you that more economic growth will fix everything, s/he is ignorant of the prevailing debt of the typical American family. More likely, they are looking for another two- or six-year term with a guaranteed salary—paid by you, the taxpayer.

Nearly one-third of the world's population makes less than $2 per day, and the world's 100 wealthiest people are worth more than the poorest three billion. A statistic regularly thrown about but factually correct. That is because we have managed to impose the rigors of capitalism on the average worker, and the benefits of socialism for the very rich. This is what happened during the Great Recession (2008) as many over-leveraged homeowners were left destitute, but the overly leveraged banks were saved. This is crony capitalism gone wild. Wikipedia defines crony capitalism as: "an economy in which businesses thrive not as a result of risk, but rather as a return on money amassed through a nexus between a business class and the political class."

Maybe even more infuriating is our bailing out the banks yet ignoring a whole generation of student debt burdening many of our young people for the rest of their lives, including hindering the basics of qualifying for a car loan or mortgage. This is an injustice of historic proportions.

What are some of the questions working families should be asking?

1. When our opiate crisis obliterates thousands of communities across our country, why do the pharmaceutical companies continue to participate in deciding elections?

2. When the wealthy can buy their children's admissions to colleges and when our representatives' time is spent courting the rich for their re-elections, how does this reinforce our democracy?

3. Why do we allow our representatives to send our minorities to jail for 20 years for possessing a few ounces of marijuana and other minor infractions? Disproportionate sentences for marijuana possession hit black communities the hardest.

4. Why do we give the very best healthcare to only those who can afford it?

5. How is it that the large corporations demand investment guarantees at the expense of the average taxpayer and small investor?

6. Why does the U.S. have the highest rate of incarceration in the world? We have about 5 percent of the global population but hold nearly 25 percent of the world's prisoners.

This is when the system is exposed as corrupt, and those who attend the "Make America Great Again" rallies should understand that with our present leadership in the White House, life, for them, will only get worse.

For the last ten years, the economy was doing well if you were a stock investor, and unemployment was 3.5 percent if you included the great number of minimum-wage earners, and inflation was low if you didn't include college education, healthcare, or the recent and unprecedented pandemic stimulus program.

Things have now changed, and the working family's plight is even worse with the onslaught of the COVID-19 pandemic ravaging our country. Trump's lies, corruption, and bigotry did not deter the undying loyalty of his followers. Still, it will be the record 16 million jobless claims statistic that came out three weeks after the start of the COVID-19 pandemic, almost twice the net job losses for the entire 2007-2009 recession, that will awaken the working family to understand they have been conned. If you are a person of color, the statistics become more ominous. In New York City, the U.S. epicenter of COVID-19, 68 percent of the deaths are African American. African Americans are 30 percent of that same population.

Similarly, in Louisiana, where 27 percent of the population is black, 70 percent of deaths are African American. Chicago has almost the same statistics. This has genuinely revealed the inequities in our country where African Americans have significantly less health insurance and are more likely to have underlying health conditions, less likely to be able to work from home, and more likely to use public transportation.

Despite the $2.2 trillion CARES Act (Coronavirus Aid, Relief, and Economic Security) attempting to lessen the 21 million newly unemployed workers' despair, the working family will face a heretofore never before seen contraction of our economy. A more responsive, less irresponsible approach could have mitigated this ensuing tragedy hoisted on the American people. The ultimate fiscal and monetary stimulus could reach $10 trillion, which would be unprecedented in financial history. The consequences of this procrastination will have dire consequences for the average American for years to come.

The Trump trail is indisputably there:

"…it's one person coming in from China, and we have it under control." (January 22, 2020)

"The coronavirus is very much under control in the U.S.A." (February 22, 2020)

"We're going very substantially down, not up…" (February 26, 2020)

"No, I'm not concerned at all." (March 8, 2020)

"I don't believe you need 40 thousand or 30 thousand ventilators." (March 27, 2020).

All the while, we knew from the World Health Organization on December 31, 2019, that the virus was coming, that it was a respiratory disease, that it was person-to-person, and that it was extremely contagious.

Both South Korea and the United States had their first reported case on January 19, 2020. Their population is one-sixth of ours, but per capita mortality and the number of cases are significantly less, and their forecasted recovery is higher.

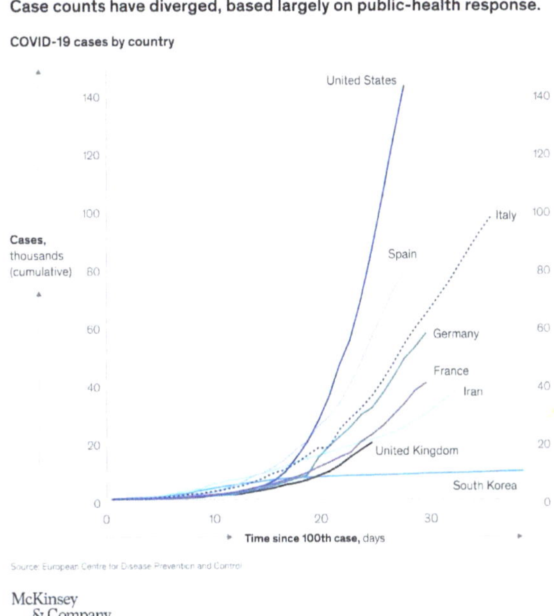

In the last three years, the current administration indiscriminately dismantled critical parts of the national security and scientific community needed for a crisis, just like the pandemic we have now. That is why we continue to lag in tests per capita (COVID Tracking Project) despite having the most COVID-19 cases in the world.

Always suspicious of science and our intelligence agencies for their independent thinking, Trump put unwavering loyalty above the expertise needed to protect the American citizen. This has contributed to a form of democracy and free enterprise alien to our history and has ultimately placed a heavy financial weight on the blue-collar worker.

We need to have capitalism based on free markets and entrepreneurship, not a fixed system where we effectively redistribute wealth to those who are already rich. Is it not logical and in the spirit of free enterprise and democracy that full-time working people should meet basic family needs? Is it democratic that the cashiers working at Stop and Shop have little political say compared to a partner at a law firm who gives to her politician's favorite political action committee? Is it free enterprise when rich folks and corporate enterprises pay a lower tax rate than the Ford foundry worker?

Every day, we hear the statistic that almost four in 10 people wouldn't be able to scrape together the cash to meet a $500 emergency expense. At the same time, more than six in 10 said losing their job would mean that they couldn't cover three months of expenses.

Another analysis from Bridgewater's Ray Dalio perfectly shows this crisis:

Real incomes have been basically flat for the average household in the bottom 60% since 1980, while they have been up for the top 40%. Those in the top 40% now have, on average, ten times as much wealth as those in the bottom 60%. That is up from six times as much in 1980.

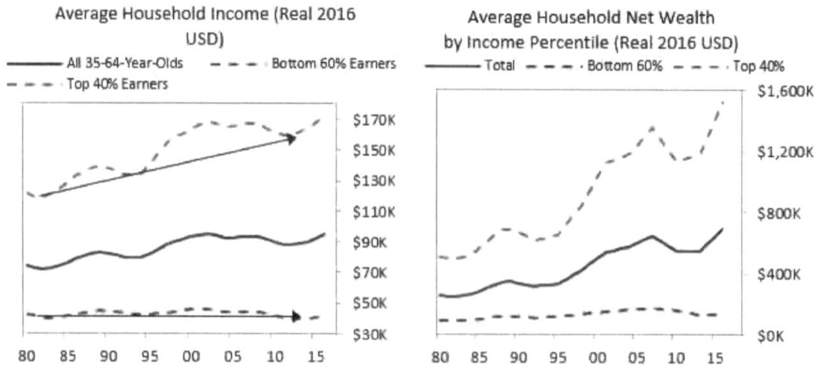

Andrew Van Dam of *The Washington Post* writes, "Amid what is likely to become the longest period of sustained economic growth on record, a new report shows that millions of middle-class and low-income Americans still aren't on solid enough ground to weather a sustained downturn." The growth rate in the U.S. accelerated in 2019 and moved down the unemployment rate (though with lower-paying jobs) but did almost nothing for productivity, as too many corporations failed to invest their increases after-tax earnings. Nothing is being done with our failing physical infrastructure, job training, or taking a global leadership role in reducing the effects of global warming. The pandemic significantly rose the ante on all the harm done to the working family over the last 30 years. For all the vaunted decline in unemployment, labor still has little ability to demand higher wages. Undoubtedly, the gig economy and the proliferation of low paying jobs that offer only 30 or fewer hours per week have caused the unemployment numbers to overstate the health of labor, something the present administration shamelessly exploited. The COVID-19 crisis will have this whole house of cards come crashing down.

These problems become compounded when we better understand the rapid change technology is having on working families. Recent advances in technology have replaced dangerous factory work or other mind-numbing labor and have initially helped worker productivity overall. Unfortunately, these recent advances in technology, where most children are trained at an early age, leave those behind if their parents can't afford to buy the technology. But as artificial intelligence increasingly becomes part of our economy's productivity, it will perform, not only the ordinary workers' tasks like grocery checkout, janitorial work, and even classroom teaching but much of what our doctors and lawyers do as well. That is, the machines will replace the activities of thinking, understanding, learning, and remembering tasks that only humans could do. So with the worker being displaced and out of a job, who will buy these products? The jobs that have been eliminated must somehow be replaced. Some are forecasting the loss of up to 50 million permanent jobs. How much worse the pandemic makes this is anybody's guess, but no doubt, we will be facing a depression until an effective vaccine is found for the COVID-19 virus.

Healthcare is nonexistent for too many, college costs are out of reach for most, and even doubling the minimum wage in most states makes providing for a family of four impossible. This will become worse as technology continues to eliminate jobs.

Many politicians are finally putting forth programs they believe will help the economic injustices inflicted on our working and middle class. Is this socialism or merely an attempt to create opportunities and correct the economic imbalance that has been borne by the working and middle class? That is, can capitalism have a level playing field?

Elizabeth Warren suggests that "If we put that 2 percent wealth tax in place on the 75,000 largest fortunes in this country, we can do universal child care for every baby zero to five, universal pre-K, universal college, and knock back the student loan debt burden for 95 percent of our students—and still have nearly a trillion dollars left over." (CNN Presidential Town Hall with Senator Elizabeth Warren. Aired 8-9p ET April 22, 2019.)

Whether you agree with her or not, it is a discussion worth having and doing the homework as to how her policies affect you. More specifically, Senator Warren's 2 percent annual tax on fortunes over 50 million dollars with a surcharge of 1 percent on wealth over one billion dollars would generate almost three trillion dollars over ten years as estimated by Emmanuel Saez and Gabriel Zucman, economists at the University of California, Berkeley. The question is, how do we implement a more equitable tax structure, and will it solve our problems? Possibly a more achievable short-term goal might be a progressive increase in estate, individual, and corporate rates with a reduction of loopholes. This, too, would benefit the working family and not face the "socialism" stigma Republicans will use as a convenient weapon in November.

As the 2020 election took full force, the democratic candidates were proposing policy proposals to try to steady the ship before it is too late. The first policy should be to rid our country of the historical aberration presently in the White House that has distorted our democratic norms and traditions. Thus, a move to the center to bring more constituencies together secured Joe Biden the nomination. Maybe the centrist call for "Medicare for those that want it" sets a better tone. The fact is, our healthcare system should not just benefit those who can afford to pay. Why do 94 percent of Canadians say that their healthcare system is a source of pride? Why do so many healthcare-deprived Americans move to Canada?

Simply put, they know that the Trump administration puts little priority on public health, and as evidenced by the disbanding of the National Security Council pandemic unit in 2018. Enter COVID-19.

The COVID-19 epidemic, better defined as the most recent global pandemic, continues to reveal Trump as uninterested in not only the health of the American family but disdainful of science as manifested by an incoherence unprecedented in his or any presidency preceding him. At first, he called the pandemic a hoax. Then, he declared that it was under perfect control as early as January 22, 2020. At the Davos Economic Forum, he added to his long history of lies and conspiracy theories he has hoisted on the American public. Besides, his call for many more testing kits was very late, and his minimizing the dangers of the virus in his news conferences ("It will all work out well." "It will go away. Just stay calm." "I'm not concerned at all.") added to the chaos and confusion Americans were already experiencing. This time, it had the immediate effect of putting millions of lives in physical danger. The testing kits are still in short supply despite the re-openings of an increasing number of states.

The Boston Globe's March 31, 2020 editorial board put it perfectly:

"What we have is a president epically outmatched by a global pandemic. A president who in late January, when the first confirmed coronavirus case was announced in the U.S., downplayed the risk and insisted all was under control…A president who, consistent with his mistrust and undermining of scientific fact, has misled the public about unproven cures for COVID-19, and who baited-and-switched last week about whether the country ought to end social distancing to open up by Easter…who has pledged to oversee the doling out of the $500 billion in corporate bailout money…some of which will go to the travel industry in which his family is invested."

The working family conned once more.

The White House's inability to manage this crisis, with no direction given to the Department of Homeland Security or the Centers of Disease Control and Prevention (C.D.C.) resulted in a total lack of investor confidence, cratering the stock market close to 30 percent from its peak in less than a month. The March 2020 stock market collapse will be ultimately worse than 2008 and 1987 despite the near 100% technology-based retracement of most indices unless the working family is better protected, and in fact, saved. The after-effects could be worse than the Great Depression. Only when pressured by the C.D.C. and numerous scientific organizations did Trump finally stop minimizing the danger for our country. But by denying the scientific community's warnings of a pandemic, damage to the working families was finalized. And somehow Trump still managed to blame CNN, MSNBC, Chuck Schumer, and Barack Obama for creating panic and his ill-prepared response team. The ability to unify the country has been lost to a Twitter hound focused on passing blame to anybody readily available.

Exacerbating this pandemic crisis is that average healthcare spending per person in the U.S. was about $11,500 in 2019, which is almost double that of comparable industrialized countries ($5,280), yet over one million U.S. citizens travel overseas for healthcare-related purposes as they are priced out of the healthcare market. Now, with the COVID-19 pandemic, the bandage will be ripped off as millions of Americans will defer going to the emergency room, seeing their doctor, even not self-quarantining when required in fear of the thousands of dollars of medical bills they would undoubtedly face. Delivery workers, cashiers, and other front-line employees are more afraid of losing their job than risking their lives by being exposed to the COVID-19 virus.

The charts below demonstrate all too well that saying we have the best healthcare system in the world begs the question, for whom? Certainly not for everyone during a global crisis. Even though a person who gets leukemia and can't afford drugs and is unemployed will certainly be facing a death sentence, that same person, if she had COVID-19 would be sent money, test for free (if, in fact, available), and be treated. All courtesy of the government. That will certainly force a difficult conversation about national healthcare and workers' rights. This is possibly the beginning of the end of government hatred started by the Reagan administration and fanned by the increasing conservative G.O.P. over the last 50 years.

Per capita healthcare spending in the U.S. is almost twice the average of other wealthy, developed countries

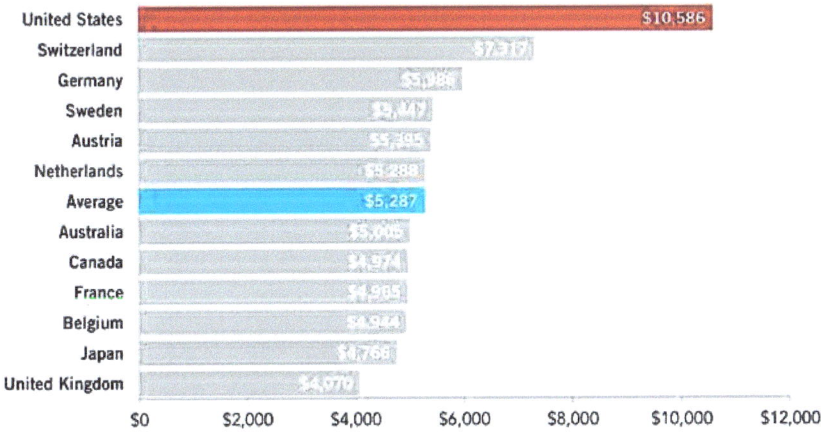

SOURCE: Organisation for Economic Cooperation and Development, *OECD Health Statistics 2019*, July 2019.
NOTES: Data are for 2018. Chart uses purchasing power parities to convert data into U.S. dollars. Average is for other wealthy OECD countries with above median GDP and above median GDP per capita.

PGPF.ORG

America's health care system is the least equal

Percent of patients who "did not get recommended test, treatment, or follow-up because of cost in the past year."

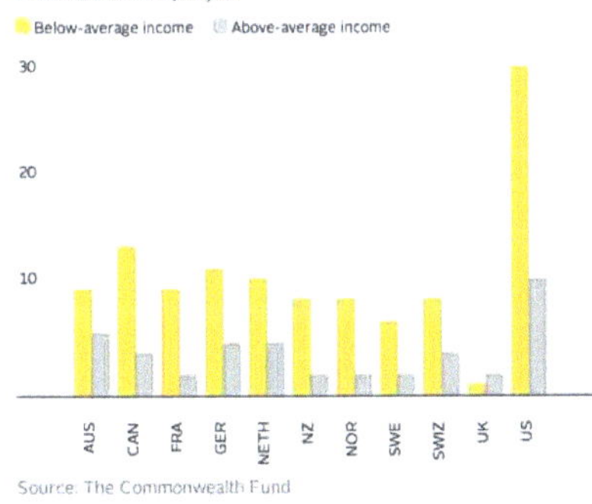

Source: The Commonwealth Fund

America has the least efficient health care system

Percent of patients who reported spending "a lot of time on paperwork or disputes related to medical bills"

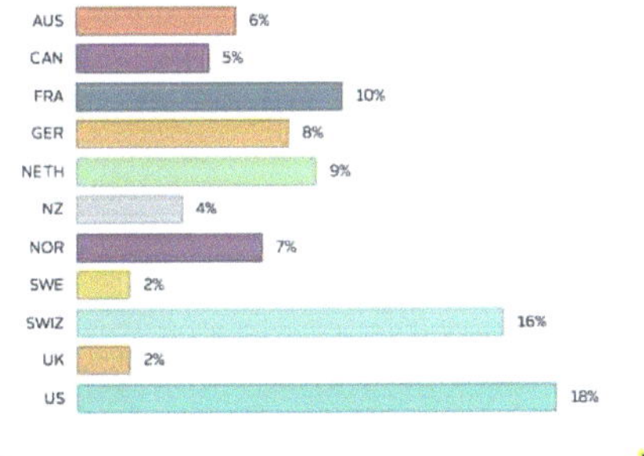

Source: The Commonwealth Fund

Chapter 3

THE BYSTANDER

"In a time of deceit telling the truth is a revolutionary act."
– George Orwell

How did one political party co-opt patriotism, religion, and the American dream? Did they fly the flag higher or go to church more? How was an administration formed that consists solely of sycophants who remain deeply in denial, and who take their direction from the likes of Sean Hannity and Laura Ingraham whose sole existence is creating right-wing conspiracies and creating a de facto state-run T.V. station?

Does God love them more? How do white evangelicals support a man who has cheated on each of his three wives, mocks our war heroes and gold-star families, discriminates against minorities and the disabled, has a lifelong history in business of swindling his vendors, is accused of money laundering, and has no sense of world history, our history, or what our Statue of Liberty stands for?

Not exactly what Christianity teaches us. Is it really about the judges and abortion? The fact is that there seems to be a good 25 percent of the U.S. (the same percentage that stood with Nixon to the end) that is willingly or unwillingly committed to racial and gender hierarchy. That's the Trump base. The next two generations have no alternative but to change that. As the economic plight of the working family continues to deteriorate significantly, the ramifications of COVID-19 will come fully into play in worsening that plight.

Elizabeth Bruening in a *Washington Post* Opinion piece asks:

"That the thrice-wed, dirty-talking, sex-scandal-plagued businessman managed to win the steadfast moral support of America's values voters, as expressed in routinely high approval ratings, posed an even stranger question: What happened? How is it possible they see this tragic figure as their protector? They tell us they know the Lord, but they act like they don't. More disturbing, they are taking their cues on how to react with their neighbors and friends from an anti-leader whose primary response is to denigrate, belittle, and mock people."

In 2014, the Pew Research Center found that 31 percent of Texans consider themselves evangelical, forming the largest bloc of religious voters in the state of more than 28 million. About 65 percent of those voters are white, 22 percent are Latino, and 8 percent are black.

Exit polls show that Trump carried 85 percent of evangelical voters in Texas in 2016. Are their values his values?

Idealizing the 1950s as a golden era for America is fantasy. Glorifying a time when our country still denied its history of racism, sexism, and anti-immigration has stymied real change.

The demographics then were different, as was our place in the world economy. Jim Crow laws were still deeply ingrained in our culture, and we were a nation that was 90 percent white.

We know we will have a white minority in the next 20 years, and as technology begins to rule our economy, more and more of our country will become disenfranchised.

On August 14, 2019, (WAPO) Les Helm and Lora Vinson, leaders in a community organizing group called Faith in Texas wrote, "I've seen a lot of evangelicals making arguments that I cannot imagine them making two or three years ago, like trying to play devil's advocate on things like the immigration policy, or locking up kids." Helm continues and believes ignoring Trump's immoral persona is "very much a devil's bargain of like—yes, he's awful; yes, he does not represent our values, but he's allowing us to pack the courts with justices who do."

Here's the bottom line. Taking Donald Trump à la carte is not in the cards for salvation or redemption.

The seriousness of Trump's moral failings and narcissistic character were justly criticized by the editor of *Christianity today* in an article written on December 19,

2019, demanding his removal from office. *Christianity Today* is not a progressive tool of the left or right. The impact of this article will become more apparent as we approach election day.

Michael Gerson, an op-ed columnist for *The Washington Post* and a registered Republican, tweets and summarizes perfectly, "Republicans are now officially the character-doesn't-count party…the deficit-doesn't-matter party, the Russia-is- our- ally party, and the I'm-right-and-you-are-human-scum party."

Bipartisanship means respectful cooperation and ultimate compromise between two political parties for the betterment of their constituents. It is creating productive discussion to achieve a synthesis of ideas. Thus, the welfare of the people always comes before party loyalty.

It's also about speaking up. "Our lives begin to end the day we become silent about things that matter." Martin Luther King, Jr.'s words are as relevant now as they were in Selma in 1965.

We face a national emergency where patriotism is now an ugly caricature, the historic majesty of our democracy is crippled, and the constant devolution of our leadership is frightening.

When will all Republicans and Democrats rally together to save our country and say enough is enough? When do they stop hiding under the false hope that things will get better? When do our local politicians stop hiding behind pothole reform? When do we finally stop averting our eyes and show our children that we will no longer walk in fear of change, that we will confront this dark period of hate in our history?

Our national disgrace is a man who dodged the draft, who shows extreme disdain for women and minorities, who maligns the free press and has no understanding of basic truth. How does this not threaten the very foundations of our democracy?

But those who remain quiet also pose a real and present danger. At some point, shame, guilt, fear, and a final distortion of our Constitution will force the silent ones to emerge. Tragically, by the time these timid souls speak up, it could be too late.

We must all protest against the current contempt for our institutions so as not to leave a legacy of cowardice for our children.

We should never allow ourselves to become numb, and we must stop the pendulum of history before it swings toward our very own dystopia.

Bipartisanship is now temporarily lost because our political and cultural divisions run deep and because the leadership in Washington has managed to dismantle any semblance of reasonable protocol. The executive branch is now our democracy's most reckless caretaker.

This means that civic responsibility to defend our democratic institutions becomes that much greater. National issues are local issues, and we cannot fear that discussion. Archibald MacLeish said, "Democracy is always something that a nation must be doing."

Kitty Genovese was an American woman who was stabbed to death outside her apartment in Queens in 1964 as most of her neighbors failed to come to her aid, thus creating the "bystander effect." We cannot be bystanders as toxic rhetoric, conflicts of interest, and lies from the White House continues almost daily. We cannot continue to conveniently look away as our democracy begs for support. Our house of decency, bipartisanship, and mutual respect is on fire.

Along with not upholding our 70-year old NATO commitments, our allies in the East and West question whether the United States could ever again achieve a global leadership role. For example, South Korea has no choice but to cozy up to China, and both Germany and France have lost the strong trust that has been established since WW2. In addition, Japan and the Baltics, front line support for the U.S. against the ascending boldness of both China and Russia, must assume much more independence than imagined before. How that will play out is anybody's guess as we assume the role of a global bystander.

Because most cities and suburbs are critically dependent on an immigrant workforce for domestic work, child care, landscapers, and our restaurants, we should protect those who make our lives that much better and care for our most precious assets. National policies have local ramifications that have to be addressed.

Have you heard your congressman defend our sisters, wives, and mothers when Trump shames women? A congressman as a bystander is not an option for a moral society needing new leadership. Vote him or her out.

Our schools speak out clearly on bullying with a policy that condemns and monitors it. Should we, as parents, not condemn the offensive ranting tweets coming from our president that demean minorities—or is he the bully we want our children imitating? Trump's cyberbullying and ad hominem attacks would get any child expelled or any employee fired at any school or corporation anywhere in the United States. There are no fake media. There is only a huckster man-child encircled by loyal sycophants who haplessly stand guard.

As importantly, what kind of moral and supportive sons do we raise when we don't exhibit our distaste for our president's innate hate of women? What kind of honorable man would accept Trump's demeaning comments to one's mother, wife, or sister? I had a mother and have a sister who fought discrimination in the workplace. All of us, with mothers, daughters, and wives, must not sit silent.

Bystanders are moving back the clock on inclusiveness, denying the good that diversity creates and damaging the century-long progress on gender equality. Please don't tell me that being a bystander is simply an instinct for political survival. It is cowardice.

We must not wait for our state and local leadership to speak out about the hate propagated in presidential tweets and speeches. We must not watch the national, as well as local waters of bigotry, continue to inch higher. If we do, we will permanently cripple our children's sense of right and wrong. It is our duty to speak out forcefully and set examples for our sons and daughters when Trump's daily hate speech is commonplace news. Is silence how we interpret the spirit of bipartisanship? Silence will not make our children responsible patriots and defenders of democracy. Patriots come from both sides of the aisle.

Teddy Roosevelt summarizes, "To announce that there must be no criticism of the president, or that we are to stand by the President, right or wrong, is not only unpatriotic and servile but is morally treasonable to the American public."

Chapter 4
FOLLOW THE LEADER

"There's nothing in the middle of the road but yellow stripes and dead armadillos."

– Jim Hightower

What creates that moment in a representative's consciousness when he or she decides to support America's historically most dangerous and unethical politician? This is especially disturbing when you realize how far we, as tax-paying citizens, have fallen in the worldwide economic food chain.

Here's what you *don't have* and all other Western democracies in the world do:

1. Properly functioning and affordable or free healthcare for the whole family
2. K-12 Education system that effectively competes with other Western democracies
3. Efficient mass transport systems for commuting in major metropolitan areas and in or across our heartland
4. Family safety nets
5. Job stability
6. Domestic security from gun violence

Why does the G.O.P. brand basic human compassion and sound public policy as socialism? These basic rights are not some perfect socialist conspiracy or revolution. They are what every American has a right to have. The con is perpetuated when the G.O.P. brands critical Democrat public policy as socialism.

It is important to understand that over the coming decade, the federal government will collect hundreds of billions of dollars fewer than previously projected. The budget deficit has jumped more than 50 percent in the last three years and is expected to top two trillion dollars in 2021, partly as a result of the tax cuts benefitting the very wealthy and the COVID-19 stimulus program—both being paid for by hardworking families.

It must be noted that the already dwindling teacher pension funds will now be further strained, and some school districts will face choices in possibly having to reduce teacher pay. Before COVID-19 began ravaging our citizens, teacher pensions were nearly 70 percent funded by the returns they made on their investments. It is now significantly lower. It is not inconceivable that in the next two years, there will be many school districts across America that will not be able to fund their pension obligations.

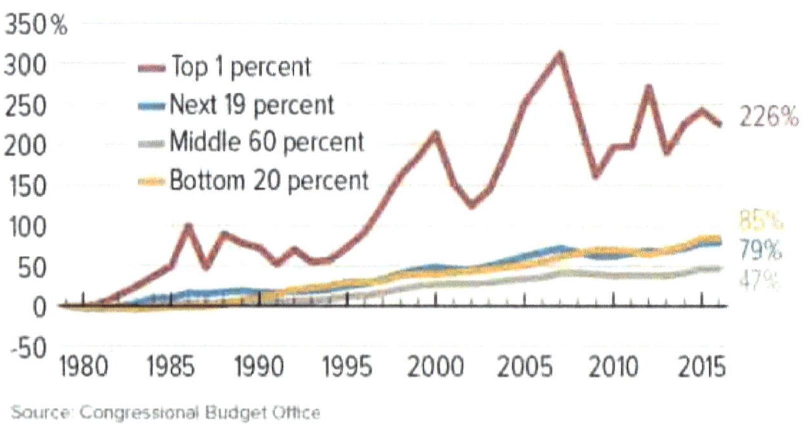

It is the latest example of the benefits of the Republican tax package flowing disproportionately to the richest of the rich. Even a tax break that was supposed to aid needy communities—an initiative called "opportunity zones"—was too often used in part to finance the gentrification of neighborhoods.

Bret Wells, a tax law professor at the University of Houston, writes, "It is largely the top 1 percent that will disproportionately benefit — the wealthiest people in the world" (*New York Times*, December 30, 2019).

The more visionary opportunity zones are investing in companies that will hire and train local residents. They enable, catalyze, and develop creative new businesses in educational technology or life sciences by bringing entrepreneurship into these zones. (The Opportunity Zone provisions originate from a bipartisan effort to incentivize private investment in low-income communities and were codified in the Tax Cuts and Jobs Act of 2017.)

The middle class is collapsing, the average American's life expectancy is dropping, and the economic pain inflicted on too many of our citizens has most Western democracies looking on in horror. The COVID-19 epidemic will only exacerbate this economic pain, given that it is many times as lethal as any seasonal flu. Our administration initially downplayed the dangers of this virus, and their late start compared to other countries in the world only hurt those most in need. This cannot be overemphasized.

The bottom 50 percent in Western Europe still possess a larger share of national income than the top 1 percent, the reverse of the situation in the United States (from World Inequality Database: WID).

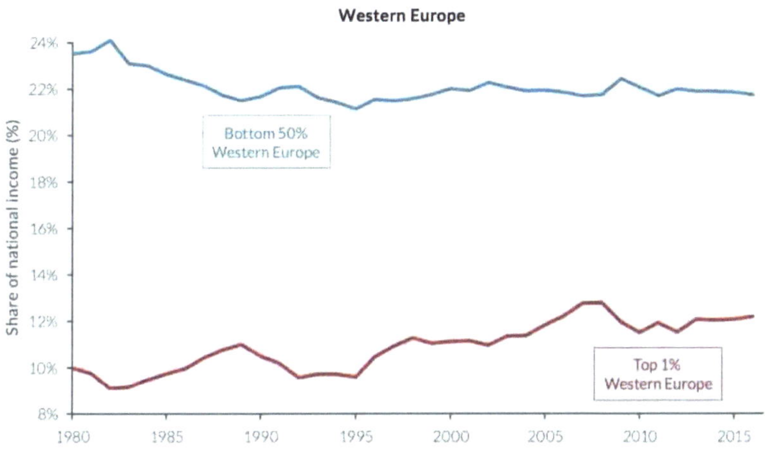

For those wanting an exhaustive read on increasing economic and social disparities, fair taxation, please commit to reading Thomas Piketty's book *Capital in the Twenty-First Century* (2013), which gives a historical perspective on income inequality in the U.S. and Europe.

Almost all Republicans continue to support a president whose hate-filled first term will most likely haunt party loyalists for generations to come. The reality is that hundreds of seemingly sane representatives have been drawn into this unrehearsed and unethical honky-tonk carnival by a self-aggrandized and racist ringleader. The bar could not get any lower for those congressional representatives who crawl alongside this demagogue's exclusionary rants simply for the convenience of party loyalty and money. The problem is there is no executive loyalty.

The *New York Times*, on December 30, 2019, made the obituary of the great G.O.P. clear, "The Republican Party degenerated into a cult, converted cruelty into public policy and normalized racism. Internationally, U.S. retrenchment ushered in a heyday for authoritarian aggressors and a dismal period for international human rights and press freedom."

Sadly, while there is outrage, not enough Democratic representatives are speaking up, in hopes of a November victory. Even fewer Republicans have tried to break their party's destructive descent into the belly of the beast by at least occasionally rejecting this demeaning and demagogic leader's daily comments.

Understanding the real economic and social issues affecting America's middle class, let alone the working poor, is critical in moving forward and making positive changes in their lives.

Meanwhile, Trump's blocking Democratic efforts to access his finances—through closeting his tax returns and lawsuits against outside entities—may be about obscuring foreign financial entanglements, including money laundering, an apparent target of continuing Democratic investigations.

Trump continues to refuse to acknowledge the Russian cyberattacks ever happened because so doing would diminish his victory. Worse, this has cramped the government's efforts to combat the next attack. William Barr, our current attorney general, is helping to quasi-validate this while minimizing Trump's corrupt and likely criminal efforts to bury it. Barr's sole agenda is to protect and massively increase presidential power and to effectively allow few, if any, constraints on this power by actually launching an investigation of the F.B.I.'s and the intelligent agencies highly evidenced-based pronouncement that Russia interfered in the 2016 election on Trump's behalf. Barr's political history, from the night classes he took at George Washington University law school to becoming attorney general, has been pushing the notion that Congress is nothing more than an unnecessary encroachment on the presidency.

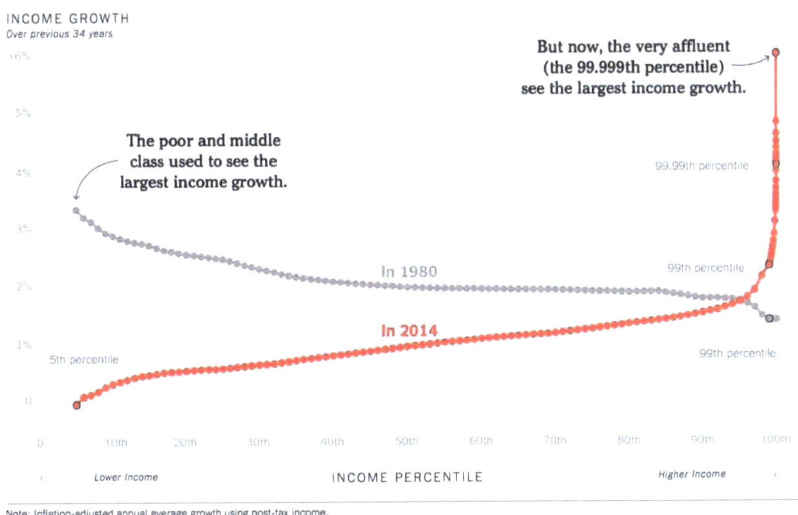

Our Broken Economy, in One Simple Chart,
By David Leonhardt, New York Times
August 7, 2017

Yet, Bob Mueller, as special counsel investigating Trump's corruption and abuse of power, stated, "This report does not conclude that the president committed a crime, it also does not exonerate him." Yet Barr followed up when he opined that the president is not acting in a corrupt manner if he attempts to influence a proceeding in which his conduct is being scrutinized.

Unfortunately, some in this economically disenfranchised group support this unstable, conspiracy-driven president, who has raged against almost every minority in our country and who has effectively practiced a life of exclusion.

To make matters worse, a slowdown in economic growth struck hardest in areas that ended up supporting Trump. The manufacturing sector, which Trump said he would save, is in a veritable recession, and is, along with much of the service industry, becoming destitute as we battle COVID-19.

Those counties (close to 3,000) that backed Trump saw annualized growth register a mere 1 percent on average, and just under half of them experienced a steep four-point percentage drop. Even worse, where there is strong Trump support, the small towns and rural counties, a widening economic gulf versus large cities in urban areas continues to emerge.

Whether Trump is rewriting American history, placating white supremacist support, inciting violence with hateful third grade twitter rants, or putting American lives in danger in the face of a pandemic, we all face what could become a permanent national nightmare should he be re-elected in November.

Our next president must be a moral force bringing all ethnicities and races together, not a destructive catalyst inciting divisiveness. Those who have been unwillingly drawn into the exploitation of the decades' long misery of the working and middle class forget that false prophets and cheap promoters always overpromise and underdeliver.

Senators, members of Congress, and state legislators must also fight the dangers of bigotry, extreme economic disparity, and understand the difficulty, so many families have in making ends meet, even in high-income towns, like Summit, New Jersey, or Greenwich, Connecticut. They must also speak out for women's health rights without equivocation.

The ironic fact is that we have elected a president who hates the working man as well as the disappearing middle class. He is the epitome of the entitled rich kid looking with genuine contempt at the 99.9 percent of Americans who haven't risen to his economic stature, an economic stature that was simply handed to him. This is a president who, for ten weeks, insisted that COVID-19 was a harmless flu that would simply disappear, leading retrograde governors like DeSantis from Florida to fail to close Florida coast beaches until late March. Finally, a president who put his smug, unaccomplished, and entitled son-in-law in charge of the medical supply chain.

Those representatives in Washington who have surrendered their morality know that Trump is a compulsive liar, that he is unread, coarse, and mean-spirited. They have witnessed his contempt of women, his mocking of the disabled, his open disdain of the media, his near-psychotic braggadocio, and his daily and outrageous slurs against ethnic religious and racial minorities.

They also know that President Trump, who has little real knowledge about our role in the world, denigrates our closest allies and has almost no real critical understanding of America's financial markets. The United States' role in the world is best strengthened by how we manage our own democracy, how we manage our relationships with allies, and by promoting global trade. At this point, we are zero for three.

The recently instituted trade tariffs will also contribute to the crippling of the working family. In the *Washington Post* on May 16, 2019, David Lynch explains the reality of tariff wars. "Once in place, the tariffs would cost the typical family of four nearly $2400 annually, destroy 2.2 million jobs and shave more than $200 billion from the size of the economy, according to a study for an anti-tariff group by Trade Partnership Worldwide, a Washington-based consultancy." Try talking to a salesperson at a furniture shop who, in 2019, earned half of what she earned in 2016 due to the tariff wars or a business depending on textiles from China who can no longer compete. No president since the 1930s has effectively taxed the consumer through tariffs like this administration.

Chapter 5

CRONY CAPITALISM AT ITS FINEST

"Better never means better for everyone…It always means worse, for some."

– Margaret Atwood

Work hard, get paid, and thrive. That's the way the system is supposed to work. If you're not succeeding, according to this logic, you're simply not working hard enough. Understand this: you are part of a system that keeps the rigid lines between rich and poor. As a struggling single head of a household or two working people raising a family, reducing taxes on corporations and the rich does not benefit the working or middle class in any meaningful way. If you work full time, you should be able to provide for your family. It's that simple. Those who advocate tax cuts for the wealthy and reductions to social programs are not only subverting the American dream but also how a fair capitalistic system should work.

The reality is that for many Americans, long hours and an unrelenting dedication to their jobs is not enough to save them from unwarranted debt, nor does it give them the ability to own a home, send their children to college, or obtain proper healthcare coverage.

In 2018, the world's 2,600 billionaires saw a 12 percent increase in wealth, according to a report by the development charity Oxfam, while the world's poorest half saw an 11 percent drop in wealth. In the United States today, the three wealthiest Americans hold more wealth than the bottom 50 percent of the country. That is a grotesque manifestation of a runaway mercantilist state ignoring and exploiting its labor force.

The prolific John Cassidy in *The New Yorker* writes:

"The Republican Party, with its eyes on November 2020, and with encouragement from Trump, said to heck with the deficit and the debt. The Republican Party leadership called time on fiscal conservatism… Under the Bipartisan Budget Act of 2019, which the House passed in July 2019, discretionary spending on defense and non-defense programs will rise by more than three hundred billion dollars compared to current law; the debt ceiling will be raised; and, according to the Committee for a Responsible Federal Budget, the national debt will grow $1.7 trillion over the coming decade."

Since the COVID-19 pandemic has torn through this country, those numbers will most likely be much worse.

History has proven that G.O.P.'s devotion to fiscal conservatism was a sham and never a true expression of their core philosophical principles. A decade of easy money has left the world with a record $250 trillion of government, corporate, and household debt. That's almost three times global economic output and equates to about $32,500 for every man, woman, and child on Earth.

Chris Wallace, in a February 2020 interview on Fox New Sunday with Rick Mulvaney, acting chief of staff and director of Office and Management and Budget, (fired by tweet from both positions in March) notes: "The deficit has increased by 15% in President Trump's first two years. By the end of his first term, that increase could be approaching 30 percent.

Somehow, this statistical fact will also be denied because in the Trump world, the more often you repeat a lie, the truer it becomes.

<h1 style="text-align:center">Chapter 6</h1>

HISTORY DENIED

> *"Courage is the ladder on which all other virtues mount."*
> – Clare Booth Luce

The last four years have been unprecedented in American politics as our national conversation continues to become increasingly disrespectful, ugly, and defamatory. Minorities are being disparaged, and families are being separated simply for who they are by Washington policy objectives that would be considered cruel as well as illegal.

We can all reasonably agree that the source of our highly dysfunctional politics is the chaotic and shockingly unenlightened White House. A recent example is the support of a Supreme Court candidate, Brett Kavanaugh, who demonstrated an angry, juvenile, and indignant "I like beer" rant when accused of sexual misconduct from several witnesses going back as far back as high school.

Regrettably, the formerly great G.O.P. and too many of its members have turned fearful and sycophantic and are still, disturbingly, in approval mode, all falling in line with chief sycophant Mitch McConnell. Many of their representatives have been neutered by their ambition and have lost the ability to put country (and budget) first. Still, several wealthy donors have kept their distance and held on to their money and their reputations. Finally, many are simply ashamed and regret their party's degradation.

I think we can agree that it won't get any better unless we vote out of office those who are, or even who might be, too meek and cowardly to speak up for the disenfranchised. Conversely, we have to vote for those candidates who can hear all our voices, those who believe the economy should grow out, not just up.

Yes, we need representatives that fight for our local schools, understand balanced budgets, and demand that we keep our police and fire departments strong. But none of this matters if the conduct of our leaders in times of crisis, both nationally and locally, diminishes our most important asset: talking truth. We need representatives who are in touch with the whole community, are sensitive to conscious and unconscious biases, and maybe every once in a while know how to disconnect from their own experiences because "we all do better when we all do better" (Paul Wellstone in a 1999 speech to the Sheet Metal Workers Union).

Though America has entered an era of uncertainty with dark threats to our existing democratic institutions, which were built by strong-willed men and women over a period of almost three centuries, there is hope this election year.

Our moral courage is going to be truly tested, and we, the people, will be challenged every single day like never before in our history. This new era of politics will go far beyond the spineless reflex of party loyalty. It will test the very core of our democracy and human decency.

Whether it's the unemployed welder who heard the siren song of a reinvigorated manufacturing base or the debt-burdened family that was promised relief, the multitude of promises that have been made all evaporated.

President Trump offered up the government and unions as the working man's enemies, and it worked. With that fear came an even larger number of hateful comments, which are now embedded into our political D.N.A. It might take generations to revert to the gene structure of a free, respectful, and open society.

A campaign with false promises and unclear change for the working man will certainly be forgotten and, in fact, denied. Populist and isolationist rhetoric that invigorated a suffering middle America will once again be twisted to ultimately benefit an increasingly smaller elite.

An era of manipulated reality could be our new political framework, which will be weaker and more vulnerable to weakening our democracy. This manipulated reality extends into our present COVID-19 crisis, where 30 percent of Americans in an April Pew poll believe the coronavirus was manufactured in a lab. This type of deception will be our new political reality unless we quickly pull the covers off the monster hiding underneath before November 2020. There is no better way to do this than for all of us to become active in local and state elections.

We Americans are sentimental people, and we desperately want to believe our leaders and their promises. The aspirations we have for our children and the hope for a better future pervades our very psyche and is the core of our humanity. We are also an optimistic and forgiving people. But if our continuous forgiveness is not met with redemption, and maybe even demonstrable humility, then we will never forgive again. Redemption is the essence of so many religions, and it is part of all our collective psyches.

"Make America Great Again" was supposed to mean that there would be better jobs, better public schools, improved healthcare, and more disposable income. It meant increased economic growth with lower taxes, less irrational regulations, and significant fiscal spending on a crumbling infrastructure. The signposts so far point in the opposite direction.

We now have the largest trade deficit in American history, a federal deficit that is now over two trillion dollars and growing, thus threatening our Medicare and Medicare entitlements. Wages for the average American have stayed flat and have not been boosted as promised in 2016. In fact, income inequality has only increased. Additionally, the cuts that the corporations received have mostly been used for stock buybacks and executive pay, and there have been no tax cuts for working families or even the middle class. Jobs are not "being kept in America," and this administration's trade wars have encouraged many companies to move their production overseas.

Finally, instead of draining the swamp, Washington, D.C. has become even more putrid and rotten. How do you put a former coal lobbyist as the head of the Environmental Protection Agency? This is your air, your parks, and your neighborhoods—where your children play and go to school. This administration has corrupted all three.

The working family needs investment in healthcare, education, job training in an ever-changing economy, and major infrastructure investment, so we can catch up with most of the Western democracies around the world, as well as China. Our infrastructure has been neglected, and there is no reason we should be falling behind most Western democracies when it comes to new and repaired roads and bridges, our water, and or public parks. (See chart below.)

The keys to reducing economic inequality are a more progressive tax system, an increase in inheritance taxes, and significant investment in our infrastructure, our educational system, our healthcare, and the environment.

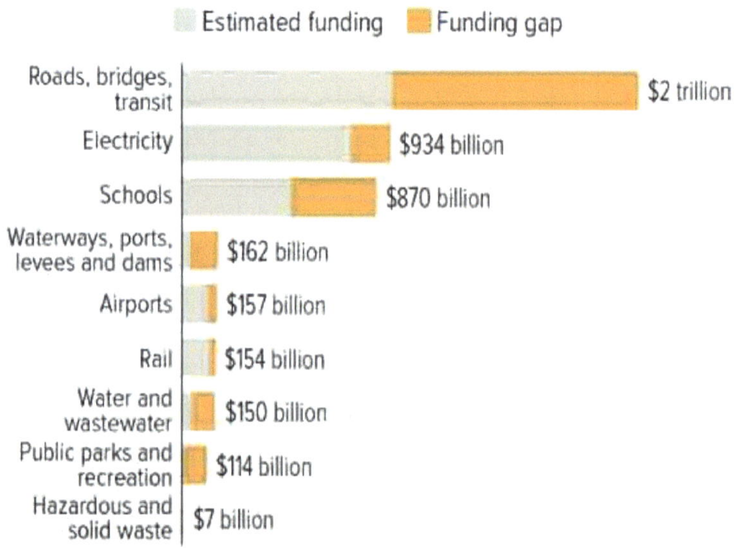

Chapter 7

YOUR LEGACY

"People seldom do what they believe in. They do what is convenient, then repent."

– Bob Dylan

"Where will the children play?" should be today's question. Our reaction to climate change is a tragedy. Nathaniel Rich from the *New York Times* makes clear that it is also a crime—

"…a thing that bad people knowingly made worse, for their gain. That, I suspect, is one of the many aspects to the climate change battle that posterity will find it hard to believe, and impossible to forgive." No doubt this aggressive, head in the sand, anti-green White House will go down in our history books as one of its most cruel, ignorant, and evil policy approaches. (Nathaniel Rich's Pulitzer Center-supported book *Losing Earth* in the *New York Times* book review.)

The Eagles in their song "The Last Resort" put it even better:

"Some rich man came and raped the land; nobody caught 'em,
Put up a bunch of ugly boxes, and Jesus, people bought 'em,
And they called it paradise, the place to be…
You call someplace paradise, kiss it goodbye."
(Source: Songwriters: Glenn Frey / Don Henley 1976)

Joni Mitchell in "Big Yellow Taxi" sang that they "paved a paradise and put up a parking lot" and asked farmers to put away the D.D.T. as far back as 1970. Finally, Al Gore nearly 20 years ago wrote:

"…For those who believed that this climate crisis was going to affect their grandchildren, and still said nothing, and were shaken a bit to hear that it would affect their children, and still said nothing, it is affecting us in the present generation, and it is up to us in this generation to solve this crisis."

If you don't believe the climatologists, then believe the Eagles and Joni. The next decade will be defined by climate change. At this juncture, our growth has to be found in creating alternative energy sources. Scientists over the last few decades have warned that unrestrained growth would lead to environmental disaster. The American capacity to create technology to produce clean energy is very powerful and where our resources should be concentrated—both to produce jobs and to protect our environment.

What we also know is that voluntary arrangements, like the 1997 Kyoto Protocol and the 2015 Paris Climate Accord, are ineffective. What is required is for every country to commit to reducing emissions and provide a way to penalize those that don't.

At a minimum, if we were taxed in a way where the very 1 percent of the wealthy were paying their fair share, this country would have much better roads and bridges, higher-quality public education, and an affordable health care system with an environment where we would not be worrying about how our children and grandchildren will survive or, in fact, breathe.

Below is a pie chart of the countries with the largest share of CO2. On a per-capita basis, we are the biggest polluters.

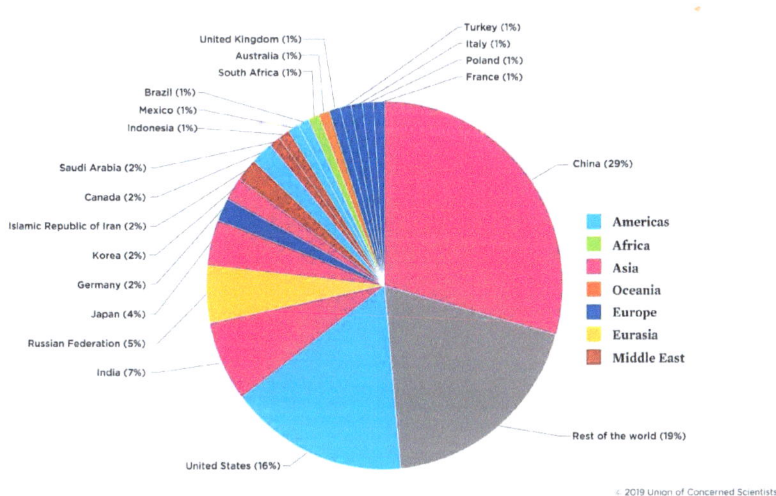

From: Union of Concerned Scientists

Chapter 8

TRUTH, JUSTICE,
AND THE AMERICAN WAY

"Life shrinks or expands in proportion to one's courage."
– Anais Nin

Republican Senator Lindsey Graham, Trump's most loyal pet, had it right in 2015 when he described candidate Trump as "race-baiting, xenophobic religious bigot," when campaigning for the G.O.P.'s presidential nomination. Now, Senator Graham is an integral part of the swamp. Only time will tell the real story of his radical about-face as Trump's biggest cheerleader.

With the reality of increasing income inequality, a struggling middle class, and an almost total distrust of our leaders, populist movements will proliferate. When more and more of the middle class believes capitalism is unfair or "rigged," our free enterprise system will collapse under the weight of this increasing income inequality. This is not the fault of immigrants and refugees who are an integral part of our heritage. They, and not our president, will continue to make this country great. Demonizing immigrants and refugees only incites fear and distracts the American public and is part of the strategy that continues to con the working man and woman who unabashedly believe his every lie.

As important is understanding who our president is. We all have a psychological profile, mostly normal. But there is a sociopathic profile for Donald

Trump that I believe few objective observers could doubt: the pathological narcissist.

"Lies roll off the tongue of a narcissist as smoothly as butter melting on hot bread. For him, lying is as natural as breathing. Even a trained observer, a therapist, can be fooled by these lies. A lie is a handy tool the narcissist uses to enhance and protect the image he has so painstakingly built. Lies are automatic; they flow from him as effortlessly as sweat coming through pores. The narcissist often believes his lies. For him, there is no ultimate objective truth, only his carefully crafted version of reality…The narcissist is not burdened by this fear. He knows he can lie and get away with it." (Excerpt From: Linda Martinez-Lewi. *Freeing Yourself from the Narcissist in Your Life.* TarcherPerigee, 2008-01-10. iBooks)

Most working families in America are dedicated to their families and to their communities. They have compassion and have friends who are suffering from extreme discrimination. Many have relatives who are in desperate need of healthcare, are married to an immigrant, have a son or daughter who is gay, have been a victim of gun violence, or are worried about their drinking water. What we know now is that we are a country that deserves better.

At the end of the day, we are a giving country. Alberto Rios, an American poet, puts it beautifully: "We give because someone gave to us. We give because nobody gave to us."

Below, the median American worker's income, adjusted for inflation, has barely changed in this century.

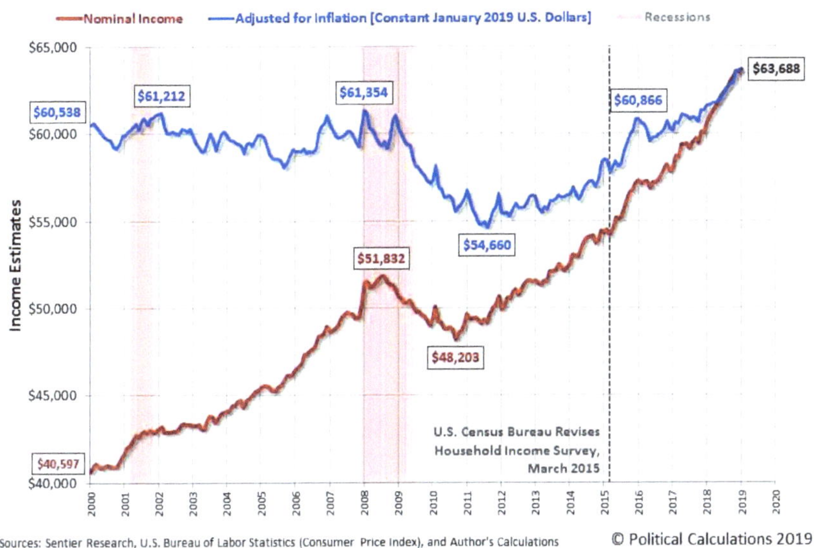

Median Household Income in the 21st Century:
Nominal and Real Estimates, January 2000 to January 2019
Nominal Income
Adjusted for Inflation [Constant January 2019 U.S. Dollars]
Recessions
Income Estimates
$65,000
$60,000
$55,000
$50,000
$45,000
$40,000
$60,538
$61,212
$61,354
$60,866
$63,688
$54,660
$51,832
$48,203
$40,597
U.S. Census Bureau Revises
Household Income Survey,
March 2015
2000
2001
2002
2003
2004
2005
2006
2007
2008
2009
2010
2011
2012
2013
2014
2015
2016
2017
2018
2019
2020
Sources: Sentier Research, U.S. Bureau of Labor Statistics (Consumer Price Index), and Author's Calculations
© Political Calculations 2019

Chapter 9

BELIEVE THE EXPERTS

"Whoever controls the media, controls the mind."

Jim Morrison

Over a year ago, way before Trump was impeached, bipartisan former federal prosecutors made a public statement that needs to be reviewed once more. It was described as a "Department of Justice Alumni Statement." It is critical this not be ignored.

"We are former federal prosecutors. We served under both Republican and Democratic administrations at different levels of the federal system: line attorneys, supervisors, special prosecutors, United States Attorneys, and senior officials at the Department of Justice. The offices in which we served were small, medium, and large; urban, suburban, and rural; and located in all parts of our country.

Each of us believes that the conduct of President Trump described in Special Counsel Robert Mueller's report would, in the case of any other person not covered by the Office of Legal Counsel policy against indicting a sitting President, result in multiple felony charges for obstruction of justice.

The Mueller report describes several acts that satisfy all of the elements for an obstruction charge: conduct that obstructed or attempted to obstruct the truth-finding process, as to which the evidence of corrupt intent and connection to pending proceedings is overwhelming. These include:

- The president's efforts to fire Mueller and to falsify evidence about that effort;
- The president's efforts to limit the scope of Mueller's investigation to exclude his conduct; and
- The president's efforts to prevent witnesses from cooperating with investigators probing him and his campaign."

"If we had confidence after a thorough investigation of the facts that the president clearly did not commit, we would so state. Based on the facts and the applicable legal standards, however, we are unable to reach that judgment." (Bob Meuller, Special Counsel)

We voted in a president whose presidential campaign was in repeated contact with Russian officials for reasons that are not totally clear, though there is much we have learned about Russian banks guaranteeing his loans from German banks. That has yet to unravel.

How can the working family in the country be surprised or shocked by the revelations about White House corruption that are revealed almost daily? President Trump may have benefited by the steady drip of news stories he has so loudly criticized in his tweets that are part of the 17,000 lies he has uttered since taking office. This is a president who has dismantled the federal government's needed national security and scientific bureaucracy, is suspicious of science and has presided over what many call a blue-collar bust. This bust will become apparent well before November when 25 million jobs will disappear undermining the trust and hope the working family had in what is now an ill-prepared response to not only an effective COVID-19 but also to just about every word that has come from the White House since January 20, 2017.

Renato Mariotti on April 19, 2019 in *Politico* writes:

"Mueller's report detailed extraordinary efforts by Trump to abuse his power as president to undermine Mueller's investigation. The case is so detailed that it is hard to escape the conclusion that Mueller could have indicted and convicted Trump for obstruction of justice—if he were permitted to do so. And the reason he is not permitted to do so is very clear: Department of Justice policy prohibits the indictment of a sitting president."

And Walter Dellinger, an acting solicitor general during the Clinton administration, tweeted, "Everyone agrees a president can be indicted once he is out of office. That (in addition to impeachment) is a reason to gather the evidence now while docs are available and memories fresh."

Justice was denied on January 31, 2020, when our Senate refused to allow witnesses at Trump's impeachment trial, and our Constitution was denigrated. Trump is simply accusing his critics of the same crimes and misdemeanors that they are accusing him of. That has been his lifetime modus operandi.

Jeffrey Toobin, in a June 29th, 2020 New Yorker article explains. "Mueller had an abundance of legitimate targets to investigate, and his failure emerged from an excess of caution, not of zeal. Especially when it came to Trump, Mueller avoided confrontations that he should have welcomed. He never issued a grand-jury subpoena for the President's testimony, and even though his office built a compelling case for Trump's having committed obstruction of justice, Mueller came up with reasons not to say so in his report. In light of this, Trump shouldn't be denouncing Mueller - he should be thanking him."

How is it possible that this was either not read or blatantly ignored by cowardly G.O.P. senators who, bizarrely, terrified of Trump, have already decided to acquit?

It is important to understand how our American democracy works.

Both articles of impeachment passed on December 18, 2019, in the House of Representatives, meaning Trump was impeached. The article on abuse of power passed 230 to 197, and the one on obstruction passed 229 to 198. But he was not removed from office. The Senate determines whether that will happen.

Amber Phillips of the *Washington Post* (January 18, 2020) summarizes below:

"The Constitution requires senators to serve as jurors to decide whether to convict the president and remove him from office on charges made by the house through articles of impeachment: in this case, abuse of power and obstruction of Congress.

Each day of the trial, they will enter the Senate chamber, surrender their cell phones, and take their seats.

They will hear opening arguments from both sides. Impeachment managers from the house will prosecute the case against Trump, and a number of White House and private lawyers will defend the president.

After the arguments are presented, senators can ask questions of each side, but only in writing. Chief Justice John G. Roberts, Jr., who is presiding over the trial, will read them out loud, and Trump's lawyers or House prosecutors can answer them.

After all that, the Senate will vote on whether to continue the trial and let both sides subpoena witnesses or whether to end the trial and vote on whether to convict or acquit the president for each impeachment count."

Here is the path the Senate actually took:

- Needed: 67 of 100 votes needed to convict. (Only 47 voted to convict.)
- There are 53 Republicans in the Senate, 45 Democrats, and 2 Independents who caucus.
- If the 2/3 (67 votes) threshold is not met, Trump remains in office. (The threshold was not met.)
- In between, there could have been votes to dismiss the trial outright. (Did not happen.)

Here's an important fact:

Majority Leader Mitch McConnell (R-Ky.) on December 17, 2019, rejected a call from Minority Leader Charles E. Schumer (D-NY) to call new witnesses during a Senate trial (*The Washington Post*). Yes, the most important trial in our nation's history had no witnesses.

Democrat Senator Schumer has said he wants people close to the president during the period scrutinized in the impeachment inquiry, such as Trump's acting chief of staff, Mick Mulvaney, or former national security adviser John Bolton (whose new revelations from his upcoming book were totally damning) to testify. McConnell wanted no witnesses at all, and the pressure by Trump worked. At trial, no new evidence was permitted, no witnesses. A part of our democracy died on February 1, 2020.

Minutes after the vote, House Speaker Nancy Pelosi (D-Calif.) told reporters she wouldn't be naming House managers until she saw the parameters of the Senate trial and was assured it was fair, strongly suggesting that she believes a fair trial includes witnesses. That didn't work.

There was no amount of evidence that could convict Trump, due to the cowardice of almost every single Republican.

If Trump was convicted on even one count, the Constitution says he has to be removed from office. This never happened. The Senate Republicans (even the more moderate ones) who they had hoped would override their party's votes heard the new evidence and witnesses but failed to kick the president out of office. History will not be kind to those who rationalized their vote.

The state of our nation's historical low point is manifested by the Republican Party losing its independence, its common sense, and its honesty, possibly forever. Jelani Cobb, on January 26, 2020, describes today's G.O.P. in *The New Yorker*, "From its relinquishing of executive oversight in the Senate to its embrace of inflammatory nativism, the Party has been perilously shortsighted."

We need the working family to change the course of our devolving democracy, our misguided Republican Party, and unite the divisions that have been created between good, well-meaning American citizens. It is only the working family that can effectuate this dream.

A political blogger and childhood friend from Cleveland, Ohio, writes of our nation's ongoing tragedy, and of an increasingly immoral and unhinged White House that we can only hope is a unique historical aberration. I believe he speaks to the soul of the working family:

"The Republican party, now the Trump party, has brought sadness to my heart for our country, the people of the world, and the spirit earth itself. Still, I hope we can find a way for his hideous rise to be the final catalyst needed to help get 'We the people…' onto a more soulfully guided path into our collective future, rather than glorifying greed, and insatiable acquisitiveness as we have so flagrantly done of late."

www.ingramcontent.com/pod-product-compliance
Lightning Source LLC
Chambersburg PA
CBHW040235240726

48664CB00001B/134